BOWHUNTING
FOR FUN!

By Jessica Gunderson

Content Adviser: John Schlieman, Certified Bowhunting Instructor, State of North Dakota;
Life Member, North Dakota Bowhunters Association, Grand Forks, North Dakota
Reading Adviser: Susan Kesselring, M.A., Literacy Educator, Rosemount-Apple Valley-Eagan (Minnesota) School District

Compass Point Books ◆ Minneapolis, Minnesota

Compass Point Books
151 Good Counsel Drive
P.O. Box 669
Mankato, MN 56002-0669

Photographs ©: R. Gino Santa Maria/Shutterstock, cover (left); Gary Sundermeyer/Capstone Press, cover (right), back cover, 4–5 (all), 13 (top), 16–17, 21 (right), 30–31, 31 (top right); Réunion des Musées Nationaux/Art Resource, NY, 6; Tom Grundy/iStockphoto, 7; George And Monserrate Schwartz/Alamy, 8 (bottom), 13 (bottom); AP Images/Brainerd Dispatch, Vince Meyer, 8–9; Tony Campbell/Shutterstock, 10; Chris Turner/Shutterstock, 11; Crystal Kirk/Shutterstock, 12 (top), 47; Jeff Banke/Shutterstock, 12 (bottom); AP Images/Ames Tribune, Nirmalnedu Majumdar, 14; Gina Smith/Shutterstock, 15; AP Images/(Peoria) Journal Star, Jeff Lampe, 18 (front); Greg Ceo/Riser/Getty Images, 18–19; Joseph Gareri/Shutterstock, 20–21; Bruce MacQueen/Shutterstock, 22 (front), 45 (bottom); Jason Lindsey/Alamy, 22–23, 27; Linda Freshwaters Arndt/Alamy, 24–25; Alaska Stock LLC/Alamy, 25 (right); AP Images/The Parkersburg News & Sentinel, Jeff Baughan, 26; Racheal Moore/Shutterstock, 28; Carlos E. Santa Maria/Shutterstock, 29; Chuck Franklin/Alamy, 31 (bottom right); Sascha Burkard/Shutterstock, 32; Michael Rubin/Shutterstock, 33; nialat/Shutterstock, 34 (bottom); Lorraine Swanson/Shutterstock, 34–35; Jamie Squire/Getty Images, 36; AP Images/Richard Drew, 37; Wikipedia, public-domain image, 38; Archer's Choice Media, 39; Franck Camhi/Shutterstock, 40; Gert Johannes Jacobus Vrey/Shutterstock, 41; Kean Collection/Getty Images, 42 (top); Hulton Archive/Getty Images, 42 (bottom); Library of Congress, 43 (top); Compass Point Books, 43 (bottom); North Wind Picture Archives, 44; David McLain/Aurora/Getty Images, 45 (top).

Editor: Brenda Haugen
Page Production: The Design Lab
Photo Researcher: Eric Gohl
Art Director: LuAnn Ascheman-Adams
Creative Director: Keith Griffin
Editorial Director: Nick Healy
Managing Editor: Catherine Neitge

Library of Congress Cataloging-in-Publication Data
Gunderson, Jessica.
  Bowhunting for fun! / by Jessica Gunderson.
      p. cm. — (For fun)
  Includes index.
  ISBN 978-0-7565-3864-4 (library binding)
  1. Bowhunting—Juvenile literature. I. Title. II. Series.
  SK36.G86 2008
  799.2'15—dc22   2008008323

Visit Compass Point Books on the Internet at www.compasspointbooks.com
or e-mail your request to custserv@compasspointbooks.com

Table of Contents

The Basics

Doing It

People, Places, and Fun

Note: In this book, there are two kinds of vocabulary words. Bowhunting Words to Know are words specific to bowhunting. They are defined on page 46. Other Words to Know are helpful words that are not related only to bowhunting. They are defined on page 47.

The Call of the Wild

Imagine moving slowly through the woods. You are surrounded by nature. All is still. Then you hear movement deep in the trees. A deer comes into view. Your heart pounds wildly. You wait until the deer moves closer. Then you draw your bow, carefully aim, and release your arrow.

The thrill and challenge of bowhunting is what draws many people to the sport. As bowhunters study and stalk their prey, they feel like they have become part of nature.

Bowhunters must rely on their natural instincts as well as their skill with bows and arrows.

Let's read on and join the hunt!

For Game and Sport

Throughout history, bowhunting, also called archery, has been a means of survival. Before methods of farming and raising animals were learned, people had to hunt and gather their food. In ancient times, people used spears to kill their prey. Spears evolved into bows and arrows.

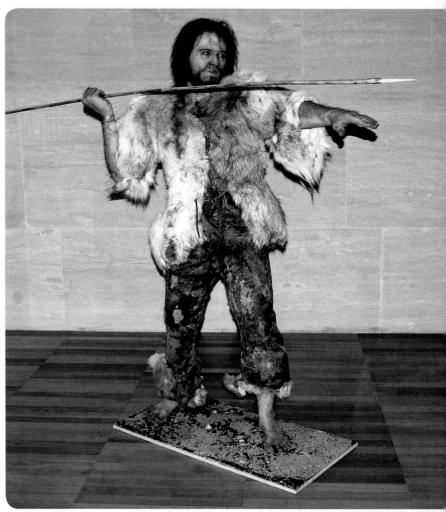

No one knows exactly when the first bows and arrows were used, but ancient cave paintings show archers on the hunt. These paintings date back at least 25,000 years. The ancient Romans used bows and arrows as weapons against their enemies. Arrows were slim enough to pass through thin slits in castle walls.

Guns were first used for hunting in the 1600s. Many hunters chose to use guns rather than bows and arrows. But in recent years, interest in the bow and arrow has risen. Bowhunters are quite common in North America.

A New Sport
In the 1600s, archery became a competitive sport, mostly in England. Competitive archery uses targets rather than living animals.

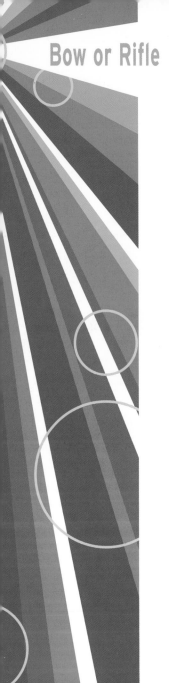

Weapon of Choice

Rifle hunting and bowhunting are similar in many ways. Both take good aim and lots of practice. Hunters of all kinds like to escape to nature and feel the wilderness around them. Often hunting season in the United States and Canada is a time for friends and family to get together and enjoy the sport.

Bowhunting requires much patience and study. If you wish to bowhunt, you must be willing to spend hours stalking your prey. You might spend whole days without seeing an animal close enough for you to shoot. You also must study the habits of your prey closely.

Although most people choose to hunt with guns, others opt to hunt with bows and arrows. A bow has a shorter range than a gun. This means that bowhunters must get very close to their prey before shooting. Animals have keen senses of smell, sight, and hearing, so getting close to them is challenging. Bowhunters enjoy this challenge.

A Big Difference

The range of a rifle is about 200 yards (182.8 meters). The range of a bow and arrow is only about 45 yards (41.2 m).

The Arrow's Target

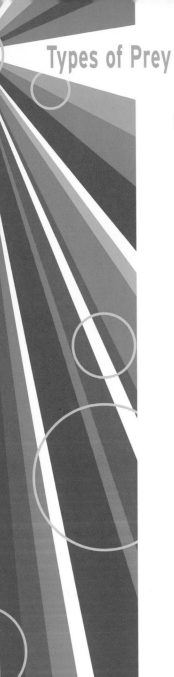

Bowhunters usually hunt for big game, such as deer, elk, antelope, and black bear. The whitetail deer is the most commonly hunted animal. Whitetail deer roam throughout North America, and their population is quite high. Many people like the taste of deer meat.

Elk is a large species of deer that is found in western North America. Elk are prized for their large antlers and flavorful meat. The pronghorn antelope is another favorite of bowhunters. Antelope are smaller than whitetail deer and usually

Elk

Wild turkeys

roam in open spaces, making it hard for bowhunters to get close to them.

But bowhunters don't always choose big game for their hunts. Small game, such as rabbits and squirrels, often are hunted with the bow and arrow. Some people even hunt for bullfrogs. Since these animals are so small, the hunt is challenging.

If you think that birds can't be hunted with bows and arrows, you're wrong. Wild turkeys are the favorite bird of bowhunters. These beautiful birds can be found throughout North America. Other bowhunters search for ring-necked pheasants. Birds in flight are real challenges for bowhunters.

Bowhunting Tools

Bow: Choosing the right bow is important. There are three basic types of bows: the long bow, the recurve bow, and the compound bow. The compound bow is the most popular, and the long bow is the most traditional. The basic parts of the bow are the riser or handle, the limbs, and the string. The limbs store the energy that propels the arrow forward.

Broadhead: The broadhead is the sharp point of the arrow. There are two basic types of broadheads. One is the fixed-edge broadhead that you must sharpen yourself. The other is a broadhead with removable blades that are already sharpened. Broadheads should be kept razor sharp, in order to cut through the thick skin, muscle, and bone of an animal.

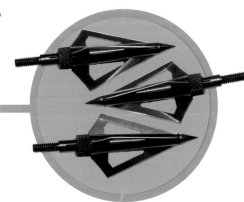

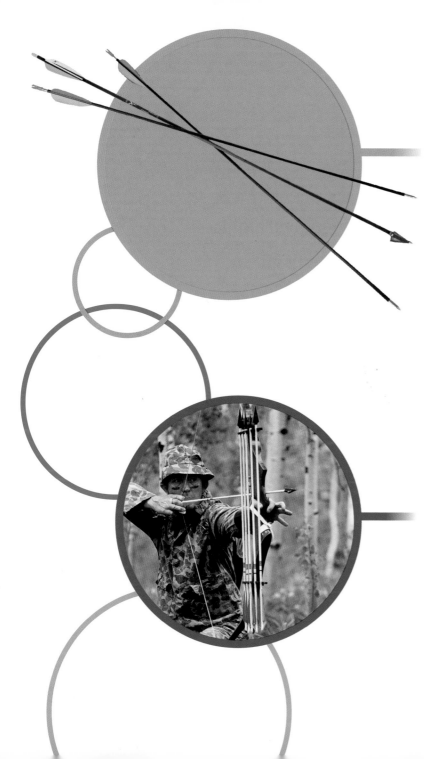

Arrow shaft: The arrow shaft is the long part of the arrow. The broadhead is attached to one end of the shaft. A nock is attached to the other end of the shaft. The nock has a slit where the bowstring will rest. Fletching—feathers close to the nock that help steer the arrow—also is attached to the shaft. Arrow shafts can be made from aluminum, wood, fiberglass, or graphite. Aluminum and graphite are the most popular. The type of arrow shaft you choose will depend on the broadhead and bow that you are using.

Quiver: The quiver is the arrow carrier. You must use a quiver to carry your arrows quietly, safely, and securely. Most quivers are fastened to the bow, but some can be strapped to a hunter's back or hip. Keeping your arrows close at hand is important so you don't miss a good chance to shoot.

Take a Class

Bowhunting is a skill that can't be learned overnight. A beginner must practice often. Even experienced bowhunters must practice to keep their skills sharp.

Proper training is vital to becoming a good bowhunter. Classes are offered through many state conservation departments. These classes cover technique as well as wildlife study, hunting rules and laws, and safety. Learning good habits and skills right away will help you become a better hunter for life.

The bow and arrow is a complex weapon. Beginning bowhunters should learn the basics of the bow and its functions before starting to shoot.

Practice, Practice, Practice
Bowhunters learn by aiming at various targets. Bowhunters need a lot of practice using their bows and arrows before they go into the wild and hunt live animals.

Choose the Right One

Long bow (from left), recurve bow, and compound bow

Finding the right bow for you is one of the most important parts of bowhunting. Archery shop employees are usually trained to help you choose a bow. Sometimes you can practice shooting before buying a bow. Be sure to ask for help if you want to try out a piece of hunting equipment.

The type of bow you choose depends upon what you like. The recurve and the long bow are more traditional than the compound bow, but most shooters begin with a compound bow. The traditional bows require much more time, effort, and practice.

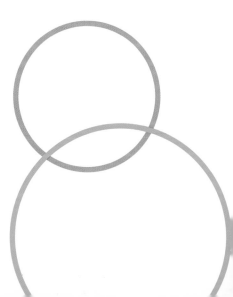

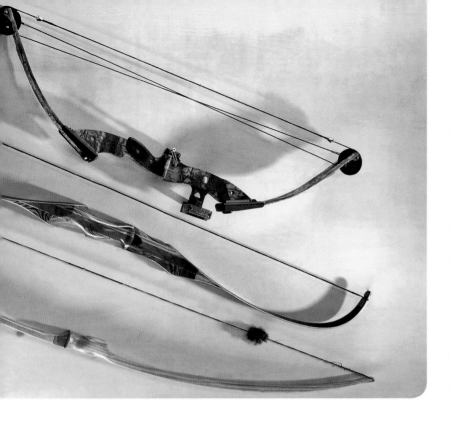

The long bow is the most traditional type of bow. It is a long, straight bow with a handle in the middle. The recurve bow is similar to the long bow, but the limbs are curved rather than straight. The curve allows more energy to flow through the bow, causing the arrow to travel faster. Many people choose either of these traditional bows because they like hunting with the types of bows their ancestors may have used.

Compound bows use a system of wheels and cables that work together to reduce the draw weight of the bow. The draw weight is the amount of force needed to draw back the bow. A reduced draw weight helps the archer stay at full draw longer. A compound bow shoots a faster arrow than a traditional bow does. This is another reason why many hunters choose this type of bow.

When choosing a bow, archers look at the draw weight and the draw length. They do not want the draw weight to be too heavy or too light. Draw length is the distance from the bowstring at full draw to the front of the bow handle. The most common mistake is to choose a bow with a draw length that is too long, which results in poor aim.

Practice Makes Perfect

Because bowhunting takes such skill, both beginners and experienced archers need to practice. One way to practice is to use targets. Targets range from small cardboard cutouts to full-size foam animals.

Your prey won't always be on flat ground. Practice shooting from different angles so you are ready for the hunt.

Advanced hunters often practice by field shooting, or stump shooting. They go into the woods and stalk natural objects, such as a falling leaf, a tree stump, or even a patch of sunlight.

It's important to practice shooting from different angles. Shoot from a tree stand and from the ground. Practicing shooting from difficult angles and positions will prepare you for real-life hunting situations.

Be careful when you are practicing. Always have an adult with you. Make sure you are aiming at safe targets. And make sure you know what is on the other side of your target.

The Sound of Silence

Some hunters stalk their prey rather than wait for the animals to come to them. When stalking, hunters move quietly and slowly through the area. Sometimes they take only one step every five minutes! Animals have better hearing than humans. They can hear sounds from far away. Even a small twig breaking is enough to scare an animal away.

A bear will run away if it hears a hunter approach.

Animals also have a good sense of smell. They can detect odors that are not natural to the woods. Don't use perfumes or scented soaps before a hunt.

Learning to stalk is an important part of the sport. Because bowhunters must creep close to their prey, good stalking techniques are vital for a good shot.

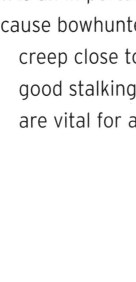

Hide Your Scent

Most hunters buy camouflage clothing that is treated to reduce human odor. Sprays that eliminate human scent are sold as well. Some hunters apply natural scents to their bodies to help cover up their human odor. Fox or raccoon urine can help mask the human scent.

Knowledge Is Key

Knowing the habits of the animal you are hunting will lead to success. Whitetail deer, for example, spend their time searching for food and water. Finding places where deer will likely go to drink, such as a creek or a lake, will help you get a good shot. Knowing what your prey likes to eat also will lead you to their gathering spots.

Animals sleep or are inactive during certain parts of the day. For whitetail deer, this is often in the middle of the afternoon. When the animals are not around, scout for places they might go, such as areas near food or water.

Follow the Food

Deer like to eat corn, soybeans, and wheat. You have a good chance of seeing a deer if you stalk the edges of fields where these crops are growing.

Follow-up

Always make sure you have a good shot before releasing your arrow. Aim for the animal's vital organs. In a deer, the most vital spot is the size of a paper plate and is found in the front half of the body. An animal should only be shot in its side. If you cannot get a good shot, let the animal walk away. If you take a bad shot, the animal may suffer needlessly before it dies.

Even if you get a good shot, the animal may not fall right away. You may have to track it through the woods. Look for trails of blood or broken branches and leaves. Be alert and cautious. If you

have made a good shot, the animal will not be far away. Do not leave the area until you have retrieved the animal.

Once you have found the fallen animal, you must do several things to preserve it. This process is called field dressing. Most animals should be dressed as soon as possible. When you dress an animal, you cut open the hide and pull out all the organs. Then you must cool the animal to keep the meat from spoiling.

Obey the Laws

Every hunter must have a hunting permit or license. In many states, bowhunters must be at least 14 years old.

Each state has its own laws and regulations. Always check the laws in your state before you begin hunting. Bowhunting season is usually longer than rifle season, but the seasons vary in each state.

To help control animal populations, limits are placed on the number of animals each hunter can shoot. In some states, hunters must buy tags. These tags must be placed on the animals after they are killed. Tags are not limited to big game. Sometimes special licenses or tags are needed to hunt birds, such as geese, pheasant, and wild turkeys.

Show Respect

When you hunt, you must respect landowners. Always get permission to hunt on private land. It is unethical and sometimes illegal to hunt on private land without permission.

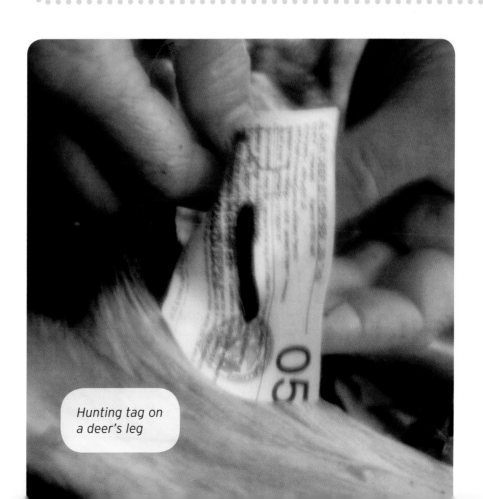

Hunting tag on a deer's leg

Play It Safe

Some people think that bows and arrows are not as dangerous as guns. That is not true. The bow and arrow is a powerful weapon. It must be handled with care. Always have an adult partner when you hunt.

Never shoot at something if you don't know what it is. During hunting season, many hunters roam the countryside. Make sure that your target is an animal and not another hunter. Always know where the other members of your hunting party are located.

Carry your equipment securely, especially arrows and sharp broadheads. Most quivers are designed to carry arrows safely and securely.

Most states offer bowhunting safety courses. In many states, a bowhunter must complete a safety course before applying for a hunting license.

Don't Hunt Alone

Beginning bowhunters should always travel and hunt with responsible adults. Hunting with a favorite adult will make the experience fun and special as well as safe.

Beyond the Basics

Tree stands: Some bowhunters use tree stands. A hunter can get a better view high in a tree. Also, tree stands can help the hunter hide from the animal's senses of sight and smell. If an animal can't see or smell you, it is more likely to come close. Two popular types of tree stands are ladder stands and self-climbers. The ladder stand is easily climbed. The self-climber allows the hunter to move up the tree as high as possible.

A hunter sits in a ladder stand.

Release aids: Many bowhunters use mechanical release aids, instead of their fingers, to release their arrows. Release aids keep fingers from getting sore. Release aids also make the shots more accurate.

A hunter uses a release aid.

Sighting systems: Sighting systems help hunters aim their arrows. There are many kinds of sighting systems. Salespeople at archery stores can help you decide which sighting system is the best choice for you.

A sighting system helps a hunter aim.

No Trespassing

Good hunting ethics help the sport survive. An ethical hunter acts responsibly and follows the rules. When hunters break the rules, their actions can lead to lands becoming banned from public use.

POSTED
PRIVATE PROPERTY
HUNTING, FISHING, TRAPPING OR
TRESPASSING FOR ANY PURPOSE
IS STRICTLY FORBIDDEN
VIOLATORS WILL BE PROSECUTED
Name _____
Address _____

When you are hunting, don't let your excitement ruin your good judgment. Always be sure of your target. Only shoot when you have a good shot. When your arrow hits an animal, always track and retrieve the creature. Leaving a wounded or dead animal is not ethical.

Woodland caribou are protected under the Endangered Species Act.

Hunting illegally is called poaching. Some forms of poaching are hunting out of season or hunting an animal that is protected by the Endangered Species Act. Poaching can cause many problems for the environment and animal populations.

Another form of poaching is hunting on private land without permission. Poachers can be punished with big fines and even jail time. Always make sure you have a license, tags, and permission to hunt.

The Good Earth

Bowhunters enjoy nature and wildlife. Most hunters are committed to the conservation of nature and the management of wildlife.

Wildlife management departments sometimes put tags on animals' ears so they can keep track of animal populations.

Hunting can help manage animal populations. If an area becomes too populated with one species of animal, the food chain can be upset. Wildlife management departments watch animal populations. They decide how many tags and hunting permits to issue each season. Hunters should never kill more animals than they have tags for. This is illegal and will harm the animal population. Much of the money that hunters pay for these tags goes toward wildlife conservation.

The wilderness is important to every hunter. You should leave an area as clean as it was when you arrived. Clean up all your gear, and do not leave any trash.

Respect Mother Nature

If you use a tree stand, make sure that the stand doesn't rip any bark from the tree.

Aim for the Gold

Archery became an official Olympic sport in 1900, but after 1920 it was dropped from the Games. In 1972, archery reappeared. It continues to be a popular Olympic sport.

There are four archery events at the Olympics: men's individual, women's individual, men's team, and women's team. Sixty-four archers compete in the men's and women's individual events. The distance from the archer to the target is about 76.55 yards (70 m). Using a recurve bow, Olympic archers shoot at both fixed targets and moving targets. Points are earned based on how close to the bull's-eye the arrow hits.

Tough Competitors
Korea has won more Olympic medals in archery than any other country.

Famous Hunters

Ishi was a Native American who spread his knowledge of bowhunting to others. He taught his friend and doctor, Saxton Pope, how to make arrows and broadheads. The two men often bowhunted together in the mountains of California. After Ishi's death in 1916, Pope and fellow hunter Arthur Young traveled to many places, such as Alaska and Africa, bowhunting with Ishi's techniques. Pope wrote

Ishi

about their adventures in a book called *Hunting with the Bow and Arrow*, which many bowhunters read today. The Pope & Young Club—an organization dedicated to bowhunting and wilderness conservation—was named after the two famous bowhunters. The important Ishi Awards are sought after by many California bowhunters.

Ralph and Vicki Cianciarulo are often called North America's favorite hunting couple. They spread their love of bowhunting with their popular television shows and informational tours. Vicki is one of the leading female bowhunters in the United States. She has shot many different species with her bow and arrow, including wild boar and alligator.

Ralph and Vicki Cianciarulo

She has even shot the blue wildebeest and ostrich in Africa. Vicki takes many photographs of the outdoors and writes articles about hunting. Her passion is getting more women and kids interested in the sport of bowhunting.

The Big Five

The continent of Africa is filled with big-game species. Some hunters go on African safaris to hunt for what are known as the Big Five—the lion, the leopard, the rhinoceros, the elephant, and the Cape buffalo.

Rhinoceroses

Cape buffalo

Dangerous Prey

The Cape buffalo, or African buffalo, is the most dangerous of the Big Five, reportedly killing several hunters each year.

The Big Five were not named for their size, but for how difficult they are to hunt. These animals are sought as trophies and not for their meat. African safaris are dangerous and costly. Hunters who go on safaris must be highly skilled and experienced.

What Happened When?

25,000 B.C.   **2000**   **1000**   **500** A.D.   **1000**   **1500**

1800 B.C. The ancient Assyrians produce the basic recurve design of the bow.

25,000 B.C. Cave drawings are made showing people hunting with bows and arrows.

454 A.D. Attila the Hun and his army use bows and arrows as weapons when invading Italy and Rome.

776 B.C. The first Olympic Games, which include archery, are held in Greece.

1337 The Hundred Years' War between France and England begins. The long bow is a primary weapon in the war.

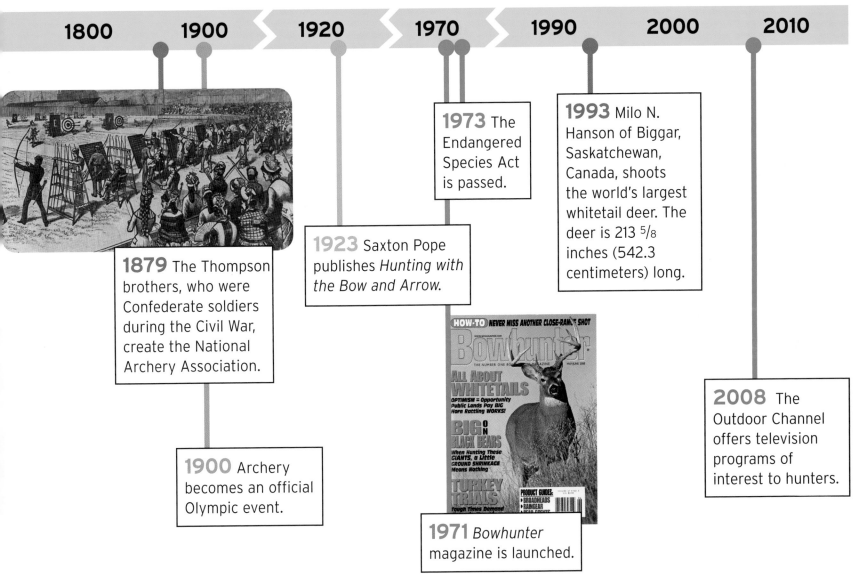

1800　1900　1920　1970　1990　2000　2010

1973 The Endangered Species Act is passed.

1993 Milo N. Hanson of Biggar, Saskatchewan, Canada, shoots the world's largest whitetail deer. The deer is 213 5/8 inches (542.3 centimeters) long.

1879 The Thompson brothers, who were Confederate soldiers during the Civil War, create the National Archery Association.

1923 Saxton Pope publishes *Hunting with the Bow and Arrow.*

2008 The Outdoor Channel offers television programs of interest to hunters.

1900 Archery becomes an official Olympic event.

1971 *Bowhunter* magazine is launched.

Fun Bowhunting Facts

The first legal bowhunting in the United States took place in Wisconsin in 1934. Before that, bowhunting was illegal or overlooked.

Native Americans usually didn't use bows and arrows to hunt bison. Instead, they ran bison off cliffs or used lances. They did use bows and arrows in warfare and to hunt smaller game, such as the black bear.

Shooting an arrow into another arrow and splitting it in half is called a robin hood. It was named after Robin Hood, a legendary archer and the subject of many folktales.

Shooting fish with an arrow is called bowfishing. Popular types of fish to shoot with arrows include carp and gar.

Wild turkeys have great eyesight. Hunters have to be fully camouflaged in order to sneak up on them. Some hunters also paint their faces. But even that might not be enough. Wild turkeys can see the whites of a hunter's eyes from far away!

Bowhunting Words to Know

archery: sport of shooting at targets with a bow and arrow

arrow shaft: long part of the arrow

broadhead: arrow's sharp hunting tip

camouflage: coloring or covering to make hunters look or smell like their surroundings

compound bows: bows with cables and pulleys

draw length: the measure of an arrow as it's pulled back into full draw

draw weight: weight required to pull a bowstring back a specific distance

endangered species: plant or animal in danger of dying out completely

field dressing: preparing a recently killed animal to cool it and keep the meat from spoiling

field shooting: practicing shooting in similar surroundings and conditions that hunters would face in real hunting situations

fletching: feathers attached near the end of an arrow

long bow: simple, traditional bow in the shape of an arc with no additional equipment attached

poaching: taking fish or game in a forbidden area or at the wrong time, or taking fish or game that is illegal to take

prey: animals hunted for food

quiver: carrier that holds arrows

range: distance between a weapon and its target

recurve bow: bow design in which the tips of the bow bend away from the archer

release aids: devices that release the arrow so a person doesn't have to use his or her fingers

safari: trip taken, usually to Africa, to see or hunt large wild animals

scouting: going into the woods or fields to find the places where prey will be

sighting systems: tools hunters use to improve their aim

stalking: moving quietly to find prey

tracking: following clues, such as blood or broken branches, to find an animal that has been shot

tree stand: equipment that allows a person to sit up in a tree

Other Words to Know

conservation: protection and management of wildlife, natural lands, and other resources

ethics: code of right and wrong behavior

evolved: changed slowly over a period of many years

hide: skin of an animal

illegal: against the law

instincts: behaviors that are natural rather than learned

traditional: referring to an old custom that is handed down from one generation to the next

vital organs: parts of the body that are necessary for life, such as the heart

Where to Learn More

MORE BOOKS TO READ

Slade, Suzanne. *Adventures Outdoors: Let's Go Hunting.* New York: Rosen Publishing Group, 2007.

Weintraub, Aileen. *The Great Outdoors: Bowhunting.* Mankato, Minn.: Capstone Press, 2004.

ON THE ROAD

St. Charles Museum of Bowhunting
Pope & Young Club National Headquarters
273 Mill Creek Road
Chatfield, MN 55923
507/867-4144

ON THE WEB

For more information on this topic, use FactHound.

1. Go to *www.facthound.com*
2. Type in this book ID: 0756538645
3. Click on the *Fetch It* button.

FactHound will find the best Web sites for you.

INDEX

ABOUT THE AUTHOR

Jessica Gunderson grew up in a small town in rural North Dakota. Some of her favorite childhood memories are of hunting season in South Dakota, where her grandparents, aunts, uncles, and cousins would gather for hunting outings. She is currently a writer and teacher in Madison, Wisconsin, where she lives with her husband and cat.